# Events

## News for every

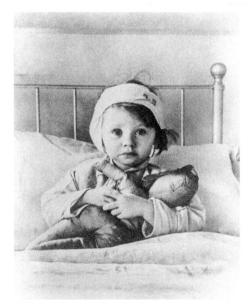

**Eileen Dunne, 3, recovers in London's Great Ormond Street Hospital after being injured in an air raid, September 1940.** *Image by Cecil Beaton.*

By Hugh Morrison

**MONTPELIER PUBLISHING**

**Front cover** (clockwise from left): A poster commemorating the Battle of Britain. An RAF Spitfire. Carmen Miranda. A British air raid warden.

**Back cover** (clockwise from top): Hitler meets Franco. A poster for the 'careless talk costs lives' campaign. Franklin Delano Roosevelt. Winston Churchill. A defiant British soldier arrives back from Dunkirk. St Paul's Cathedral in the Second Great Fire of London.

**Image credits:** Joe Dye, H. Hensser, Gauss, Queensland Newspapers Pty Ltd. Tony Foster, Jniemenmaa, National Archives and Record Administration, John N, H.E. Cook/War Office, Ed G2S, *Horticulture Week*, Brian McGuirk, H. Funk, B.J. Daventry, Bill Brandt, Ian Frederick Rose, Narodowe Archiwum Cyfrowe, Poland, Alan Light, G. Keating.

Published in Great Britain by Montpelier Publishing.
Printed and distributed by Amazon KDP.
This edition © 2019. All rights reserved.
ISBN: 9781079488487

# January 1940

**Monday 1:** The Battle of Raate Road begins in the Winter War between the USSR and Finland.

**Tuesday 2:** The government of Eire (now the Republic of Ireland) introduces emergency legislation to allow the internment of Irish Republican Army (IRA) members.

Unity Mitford.

**Wednesday 3:** Pro-Nazi socialite Unity Mitford, a member of Adolf Hitler's inner circle, returns to England from Germany under police guard.

**Thursday 4:** The Polish government in exile establishes military units in France.

**Friday 5:** Radio engineer Edwin F Armstrong demonstrates FM radio in the USA for the first time.

**Saturday 6:** Finnish ace pilot Jorma Sarvanto shoots down six Soviet bomber planes in a single engagement.

HMS *Seahorse*.

**Sunday 7:** The British submarine *Seahorse* is sunk and another Royal Navy sub, the *Undine*, is badly damaged in the North Sea off Heligoland by German minesweepers.

# January 1940

**Monday 8:** Rationing of butter, bacon, ham and sugar is introduced in the United Kingdom.

**Tuesday 9:** The British submarine *Starfish* is sunk by German minesweepers at the Heligoland Bight in the North Sea.

**Wednesday 10:** The Mechelen Incident: a German aircraft crash lands in Belgium carrying plans for the German invasion of the Low Countries; it is intercepted by Belgian intelligence.

**Thursday 11:** Howard Hawks' screwball comedy *His Girl Friday* starring Cary Grant and Rosalind Russell is released in the USA.

**Friday 12:** NBC television makes its first broadcast in the USA, with the transmission of the play *Meet the Wife* to the Schenectady area of New York.

**Saturday 13:** Mobilisation begins in Belgium and the Netherlands following the discovery of German invasion plans on 10 January.

**Sunday 14:** 17 members of the pro-Nazi radical group The Christian Front are arrested in Brooklyn, New York City, on suspicion of plotting to overthrow the US government.

**Cary Grant, Rosalind Russell and Ralph Bellamy in *His Girl Friday*.**

# January 1940

**Monday 15:** The Dutch cargo shop *Arendskerk* is sunk by the German Navy off the coast of France; all 65 crew are rescued.

**Neville Chamberlain.**

**Tuesday 16:** Speaking in the first meeting of Parliament of the New Year, British Prime Minister Neville Chamberlain says that the hitherto 'phoney' war may be about to enter 'a more acute phase'.

**Wednesday 17:** Unusually low temperatures are recorded across Europe: in London, the River Thames freezes over for the first time since 1888.

**Thursday 18:** The Palmiry Massacre: 225 Jews in Warsaw are arrested by occupying German authorities and shot dead over the course of a week in the Palmiry Forest outside the city.

Five people are killed in an explosion at the Royal Gunpowder Mills in Waltham Abbey, Essex, England.

**Friday 19:** 77 people are killed when the British destroyer HMS *Grenville* hits a mine in the Thames Estuary.

**Saturday 20:** Winston Churchill broadcasts a radio speech urging neutral countries to join the war effort on the allied side, stating that there is 'no speedy end' to the war except through unified action.

**Sunday 21:** The British destroyer HMS *Exmouth* is sunk by German submarine *U-22* in Moray Firth, Scotland, with the loss of all hands.

Golfer Jack Nicklaus is born in Columbus, Ohio.

# January 1940

**Monday 22:** A report published by the US Treasury shows that America's highest paid movie star is Claudette Colbert, with an income of $301,944.

**Tuesday 23:** Centuries of tradition are ended when it it is announced that Scottish troops will no longer wear kilts in battle, due to fears over the effects of poison gas.

**Wednesday 24:** The film version of John Steinbeck's novel *The Grapes of Wrath*, starring Henry Fonda and Jane Darwell, premieres in New York City.

**Thursday 25:** The Jewish ghetto in Lodz, Poland, is established. The photo left shows a footbridge built to prevent Jews from accessing a main road through the ghetto.

**Friday 26:** German submarines are given permission to attack merchant shipping without warning (except for Spanish, Russian, Japanese and American vessels) in the waters surrounding Great Britain.

**Saturday 27:** A savage ice storm engulfs Wales and southern England, downing electricity and phone lines and making many roads impassable.

**Sunday 28:** Finnish troops knock out invading Soviet forces at Lake Ladoga, Finland.

# January/February 1940

**Monday 29:** Actor Laurence Olivier is divorced from actress wife Jill Esmond, with fellow actress Vivien Leigh cited as co-respondent.

**Tuesday 30:** Adolf Hitler makes his first formal address to the public in Berlin after narrowly avoiding an assassination attempt in November.

**Wednesday 31:** A secret British mission is undertaken to order fighter planes from neutral Italy; the order is later blocked following German intervention.

**Thursday 1:** American science fiction writer Philip Francis Nowlan, creator of Buck Rogers, dies aged 51.

**Friday 2:** Actor and comedian Sir David Jason (*Only Fools and Horses, Open All Hours, A Touch of Frost*) is born in London, England.

**Saturday 3:** The first German plane to be shot down over England, a Heinkel HE11, crashes near Whitby, Yorkshire.

**Sunday 4:** The countries of the Balkan Pact (Greece, Turkey, Romania and Yugoslavia) declare neutrality.

**RAF ground crew clear snow from a Fairey fighter-bomber during record cold weather.**

# February 1940

A 'careless talk costs lives' poster.

**Monday 5:** The Anglo-French Supreme War Council meets in Paris to discuss intervention in the Winter War.

**Tuesday 6:** The 'careless talk costs lives' propaganda campaign against war gossip begins in the UK.

**Wednesday 7:** The Walt Disney animated feature *Pinocchio* premieres in New York City.

**Thursday 8:** The adventure film *The Swiss Family Robinson*, starring Freddie Bartholomew, is released in the USA.

**Friday 9:** Joe Louis retains the world heavyweight boxing title when he defeats Arturo Godoy in Madison Square Garden, New York City.

**Saturday 10:** Cartoon characters Tom and Jerry make their screen debut in *Puss Gets The Boot*.

The mass deportation of Poles from Soviet occupied territories to labour camps in the USSR begins.

**Sunday 11:** Author John Buchan, creator of Richard Hannay (*The 39 Steps*) and former Governor General of Canada, dies aged 64.

**Walt Disney's** *Pinocchio.*

# February 1940

**Monday 12:** German submarine *U33* is sunk in the Forth of Clyde near Glasgow, Scotland. A rescued crew member is found to be in possession of parts of the Enigma decoding machine, which are sent to computer expert Alan Turing for analysis.

**Tuesday 13:** Sweden turns down a request from Finland for military assistance against the USSR.

**Wednesday 14:** The British government grants permission for its subjects to volunteer with the Finnish armed forces.

**Thursday 15:** The Soviets are victorious in the Second Battle of Summa, over-running Finland's Mannerheim Line defences.

**Friday 16:** The crew of HMS *Cossack* seizes the German steamer *Altmark* in Norwegian waters and rescues 299 prisoners of war; neutral Norway makes a formal protest over the action.

**Saturday 17:** Erich von Manstein presents the Manstein Plan for the invasion of France and the Low Countries to Adolf Hitler, who approves the plan.

**Sunday 18:** 157 men are killed when British destroyer HMS *Daring* is sunk by a German U-boat off the Orkney Islands.

**Left: HMS *Cossack* returns to Leith, Scotland, after rescuing 299 POWs.**

# February 1940

**Monday 19:** The Finnish army successfully repels a Soviet attack at Lake Suvanto.

A Soviet prisoner of war in Finland.

**Tuesday 20:** Footballer and commentator Jimmy Greaves, Tottenham Hotspurs' highest ever scorer, is born in London.

**Wednesday 21:** A Gallup poll in the USA shows that 77% of Americans approve of military intervention in Europe to prevent a German defeat of Britain and France.

**Thursday 22:** 12 people are injured by Irish republican terrorist bombs in London's West End, the last attacks of the IRA's 'S-Plan' mainland bombing campaign.

**Friday 23:** The German submarine *U-53* is sunk by the Royal Navy off the Orkney Islands.

**Saturday 24:** Adolf Hitler leads celebrations in Munich on the twentieth anniversary of the founding of the Nazi Party.

**Sunday 25:** The first squadron of the Royal Canadian Air Force arrives in Britain.

# February/March 1940

**Monday 26:** The liner RMS *Queen Elizabeth* sails to New York to be refitted as a troop ship. A disinformation campaign convinces German spies that she is travelling to Southampton instead.

**Tuesday 27:** Carbon-14 or radiocarbon, the principal component in the carbon-dating process, is discovered by Martin Kamen and Sam Ruben at the University of California.

**Wednesday 28:** In British Mandatory Palestine (now Israel) laws are introduced to prevent the sale of land to non-arabs in certain areas.

**Thursday 29:** *Gone with the Wind* wins eight Academy Awards including Best Picture. Hattie McDaniel becomes the first black American to win an Oscar.

**Friday 1:** The adventure film *Strange Cargo* starring Joan Crawford and Clark Gable is released.

**Saturday 2:** The Hungarian Volunteer Detached Battalion departs to aid Finland in the Winter War; by the time they are able to get there the war has ended.

**Clark Gable and Vivien Leigh in *Gone with the Wind*, which wins eight Academy Awards.**

**Sunday 3:** The USA's chief diplomat, Sumner Welles, meets with senior Nazi Hermann Goering near Berlin for discussions on the European war.

# March 1940

**A woman on war work.**

**Monday 4:** The British government announces that women factory employees will not be required to undertake more than 60 hours war work per week.

**Tuesday 5:** A Finnish delegation departs for Moscow to sue for peace in the Winter War.

**Wednesday 6:** Finnish sniper Simo Häyhä, known as the 'White Death' by Soviet troops, is finally stopped (after c. 500 kills) after being badly injured by Russian gunfire.

**Thursday 7:** The USA's chief diplomat Sumner Welles meets French president Albert Lebrun for war talks in Paris.

**Friday 8:** Moscow rejects Finland's pleas for an immediate ceasefire.

**Saturday 9:** The Royal Navy releases seven Italian ships seized in the English Channel on 5 March; the vessels were attempting to transport coal from Germany to neutral Italy; a ban is placed on all German-Italian freight in the Channel.

**Sunday 10:** Actor Chuck Norris (*Missing in Action*) is born in Ryan, Oklahoma.

**Above right: Top diplomat Sumner Welles.**
**Right: Chuck Norris, born 10 March.**

# March 1940

Above: The dark areas show the territory ceded by Finland to the USSR.

**Monday 11:** As German invasion increasingly becomes likely, France transfers its 147 tons of gold reserves to Canada for safekeeping.

**Tuesday 12:** The Moscow Peace Treaty ends the Winter War; Finland cedes 16,000 square miles of territory to the USSR including the border regions of Karelia and Salla.

**Wednesday 13:** Hostilities between the Soviet Union and Finland cease at 11.00 am.

**Thursday 14:** 450,000 Finns displaced by the Moscow Peace Treaty are forced to leave their homes.

**Friday 15:** Members of the Romanian fascist party, the Iron Guard, are granted an amnesty in return for their support of the king, Carol II.

**Saturday 16:** The first British civilian is killed in a German air raid on the British fleet at Scapa Flow in Scotland.

**Sunday 17:** An all-star major league baseball game is held in Tampa, Florida which raises over $20,000 for the relief of Finland.

# March 1940

**Monday 18:** Hitler and Mussolini meet to discuss war plans; it is agreed that neutral Italy will join the war on the German side at a later date.

**Tuesday 19:** The RAF launches an attack on the German seaplane bases of Sylt and Hornum in the Frisian Islands.

**Wednesday 20:** German biologist and eugenicist Alfred Ploetz, who coined the term 'racial hygiene', dies aged 79.

**Laurence Olivier and Joan Fontaine star in *Rebecca*.**

**Thursday 21:** The film version of Daphne Du Maurier's novel *Rebecca*, starring Laurence Olivier and Joan Fontaine, premieres in Miami, Florida.

**Friday 22 (Good Friday):** 67 members of the Polish resistance are shot by firing squad by occupying German forces in Gdansk, Poland.

**Saturday 23:** The quiz show *Truth or Consequences* is broadcast for the first time on NBC radio in the USA.

The Lahore Resolution, calling for the establishment of two Muslim states separate from British India, is passed by the All-India Muslim League.

**Sunday 24 (Easter Sunday):** 28 men are killed when the French destroyer *La Railleuse* is sunk off the coast of north Africa by the accidental explosion of one of its own torpedoes.

# March 1940

**Monday 25:** The British government orders all troops captured as POWs not to take part in German propaganda broadcasts.

**Tuesday 26:** The Liberal government in Canada, led by William Lyon Mackenzie King, is re-elected.

Nancy Pelosi, Speaker of the US House of Representatives, is born in Baltimore, Maryland.

**Wednesday 27:** Michael Joseph Savage, Prime Minister of New Zealand, dies in office and is replaced by Peter Fraser.

**Nancy Pelosi.**

**Thursday 28:** The Anglo-French Supreme War Council meets in London and agrees that neither country will make a separate peace with Germany.

**Friday 29:** Samba and bossa nova singer Astrud Gilberto is born in Salvador Bahia, Brazil.

**Singer Ray Eberle.**

**Saturday 30:** *When You Wish Upon a Star* by Ray Eberle and the Glenn Miller Orchestra tops the US charts.

**Sunday 31:** Winston Churchill broadcasts his speech 'Dwelling in the Cage with the Tiger' warning neutral countries of the threat from Nazi Germany.

Paper rationing is introduced in the UK for printers and publishers.

# April 1940

**Monday 1:** BBC radio broadcasts what purports to be a speech by Adolf Hitler about his plans for the conquest of America; it is later revealed as an April Fool's Day hoax.

**Tuesday 2:** Dutch troops are mobilised on the German border.

Actress Dame Penelope Keith (*To The Manor Born*, *The Good Life*) is born in Sutton, Surrey.

**Wednesday 3:** The British government approves Operation Wilfred, involving mine-laying and other pre-emptive secret defences of neutral Norway.

**Vichy French propaganda poster about the Katyn massacre. The text reads: 'If the Soviets win the war - Katyn everywhere.'**

**Thursday 4:** British Prime Minister Neville Chamberlain announces that Germany has 'missed the bus' for an invasion of Britain after not taking advantage of military supremacy early in the war.

**Friday 5:** The Katyn Massacre of Polish soldiers by Soviet forces begins in Poland; overall an estimated 22,000 men are killed and the incident is covered up until its discovery by German forces in 1943. Germany then uses the incident to discredit the USSR which by then is on the Allied side.

**Saturday 6:** German submarine *U-1* goes missing, presumed lost, in the North Sea.

**Sunday 7:** British reconnaissance aircraft spot a large German naval force heading northwards to Denmark and Norway; attempts to stop the flotilla are unsuccessful.

**Captain Roope VC.**

**Monday 8:** The first Victoria Cross of the war is won by Captain Gerard Broadmead Roope, Royal Navy, who is killed when his ship, HMS *Glowworm* manages to ram and incapacitate the far stronger German cruiser, *Admiral Hipper.*

It is one of the very few citations that come from the enemy: the captain of the Admiral Hipper is so impressed by Roope's gallantry that after the war he recommends him for the VC, which is awarded posthumously in 1946.

**Tuesday 9:** Norway and Denmark are given an ultimatum by Germany to capitulate or be invaded. Denmark accepts; Norway vows to fight.

**Wednesday 10:** Fierce fighting breaks out as Germany invades Norway. Two German destroyers are sunk by the Royal Navy who also lose two destroyers and two submarines.

**Thursday 11:** Winston Churchill, First Lord of the Admiralty, announces that Britain has occupied the Danish Faroe Islands to prevent their strategic use by Germany.

**Friday 12:** The Cyprus Regiment of the British Army is raised, consisting of 30,000 volunteers from both Turkish and Greek Cypriot communities.

**Saturday 13:** Eight German destroyers and a submarine are sunk by the Royal Navy off the coast of Norway in the Second Battle of Narvik.

**Sunday 14:** Norwegian troops engage the Germans at the Battle of Dombas; the first British troops arrive to provide assistance to Norway.

# April 1940

**Monday 15:** The British 146th Infantry Brigade arrives in Norway; the 25-day Battle of Hegra Fortress begins.

**Tuesday 16:** The future Queen Margrethe II of Denmark (acceded 1972) is born in Copenhagen, Denmark.

**Wednesday 17:** The British ocean liner *Queen Mary* arrives in Sydney, Australia, for refitting as a troopship.

**Thursday 18:** The British 148th Infantry Brigade lands in Norway.

**Friday 19:** British and German land forces engage for the first time in the war, at Verdal, Norway. The neutral Swiss government issues instructions for mobilisation in the event of German invasion.

**Saturday 20:** Adolf Hitler orders the formation of the first Scandinavian SS unit in Norway.

**Sunday 21:** *Take It Or Leave It*, the forerunner to the TV quiz show *The $64,000 Question*, premieres on CBS Radio in the USA.

**British soldiers en route to Norway with new sheepskin coats.**

# April 1940

**Monday 22:** British troops retreat at Namsos, Norway, in the face of a numerically superior German advance.

British troops meet locals in Norway.

**Tuesday 23:** Sir John Simon, Britain's Chancellor of the Exchequer, announces record tax and duty increases to meet the costs of the war.

**Wednesday 24:** The first issue of *Batman* comic is published in the USA.

**Thursday 25:** Actor Al Pacino is born in New York City.

**Friday 26:** British troops are in retreat all over Norway, and the British government discusses a full withdrawal.

**Saturday 27:** Germany's Heinrich Himmler orders the creation of a new concentration camp at Auschwitz in occupied Poland.

**Sunday 28:** The Glenn Miller Orchestra records their hit song *Pennsylvania 65000*. The title refers to the telephone number of New York's Pennsylvania Hotel, a popular music venue.

# April/May 1940

**Monday 29:** Finland announces it will not host the scheduled 1940 summer Olympics, which have already been cancelled in the original venue of Tokyo.

**Tuesday 30:** The British sloop *Bittern* is badly damaged by German dive-bombers off the coast of Norway.

**Wednesday 1:** Chinese and Japanese troops clash at the Battle of Zaoyang-Yichang in the Second Sino-Japanese War.

**Thursday 2:** British and French troops evacuate from Norway.

**Exhausted British troops wait for evacuation at Namsos, Norway.**

**Friday 3:** HMS *Afridi* and the French destroyer *Bison* are sunk while evacuating Norway; Norwegian troops south of Trondheim surrender to German forces.

**Saturday 4:** Physician and medical thriller writer Robin Cook (*Coma, Shock*) is born in New York City.

**Sunday 5:** The Battle of Hegra Fortress ends, giving Germany complete victory in southern Norway.

Belgian refugees flee from the advancing German army.

**Monday 6:** John Steinbeck is awarded a Pulitzer Prize for his novel, *The Grapes of Wrath*.

**Tuesday 7:** Several MPs urge Prime Minister Chamberlain to resign over the defeat in Norway; Leo Amery MP quotes Oliver Cromwell's famous statement: 'in the name of God, go!'

**Wednesday 8:** British Prime Minister Neville Chamberlain narrowly survives a vote of no confidence in Parliament.

**Thursday 9:** British troops occupy Iceland following fears of a German invasion. Luxembourg's royal family and government flees to France.

**Friday 10:** Germany invades France and the Low Countries.

British Prime Minister Neville Chamberlain resigns; King George VI asks Winston Churchill to take over.

**Saturday 11:** German troops sweep through the Netherlands and Belgium, conquering Luxembourg in one day.

**Sunday 12:** Child film star Shirley Temple retires aged 12.

# May 1940

**Monday 13:** Queen Wilhelmina of the Netherlands flees to London. Winston Churchill makes his first speech as Prime Minister, stating 'I have nothing to offer but blood, toil, tears and sweat.'

**Tuesday 14:** The Local Defence Volunteers (LDV, later renamed the Home Guard) is formed in Britain. A civilian militia comprising men too old or too young to serve in the regular forces, it is intended to assist the military and armed police in repelling a German invasion.

**Volunteers of the LDV armed citizens' militia patrol a canal in Edinburgh, Scotland.**

**Wednesday 15:** The Netherlands surrenders to Germany at 10.15 am. In response to German bombing of Rotterdam, the RAF begins bombing of German cities.

**Thursday 16:** German forces break through Belgium's K-W Line series of defensive fortifications. Large scale internment of foreign nationals begins in Britain.

**Friday 17:** The Germans capture the Belgian capital, Brussels.

**Saturday 18:** Rommel's Panzer division sweeps into northern France and captures the city of Cambrai.

**Sunday 19:** Lord Gort, commander of British troops in France, orders a general withdrawal towards the port of Dunkirk.

# May 1940

**Monday 20:** German forces capture the city of Amiens in northern France, and reach the northern French coast.

**Tuesday 21:** British forces make initial gains in the Battle of Arras counter-attack but are then forced to withdraw.

**Wednesday 22:** The Emergency Powers (Defence) Act 1940 is passed in the UK, putting banks and munitions production under state control.

**Thursday 23:** Oswald Mosley, leader of the British Union of Fascists, is arrested under new defence regulations.

**Friday 24:** A failed assassination attempt by Soviet agents takes place on exiled politician Leon Trotsky in Mexico.

**Saturday 25:** German forces capture the French port of Boulogne.

**Sunday 26:** Prince Wilhelm of Prussia, grandson of the exiled Kaiser Wilhelm II, is killed while serving with the German army in France. He is outlived by both his father and grandfather.

**British troops erect anti-tank barriers outside Amiens, France, in an attempt to slow the relentless German advance.**

# May/June 1940

**Monday 27:** Operation Dynamo, the evacuation of British forces from Dunkirk using thousands of ships, many of them small civilian vessels, begins. SS forces shoot 97 captured members of the Royal Norfolk Regiment in cold blood; two survive enabling the senior SS officer to be tried and executed after the war.

**Tuesday 28:** Belgium surrenders unconditionally at 04.00.

**Wednesday 29:** 33,558 troops are evacuated from Dunkirk; the Royal Navy destroyers *Grafton, Grenade* and *Wakeful* are sunk.

**Thursday 30:** 53,823 troops are evacuated from Dunkirk.

**Friday 31:** 68,014 troops are evacuated from Dunkirk, the highest number of any one day, mainly due to bad weather making conditions difficult for German aircraft.

**Saturday 1:** German troops conquer the remainder of Norway.

**Sunday 2:** Adolf Hitler enters French territory for the first time in the war, visiting the Canadian war memorial at Vimy.

**Thousands of British troops await evacuation from Dunkirk.**

**British troops arrive in Dover after evacuation.**

**Monday 3:** The last British troops are evacuated from Dunkirk.

**Tuesday 4:** The Battle of Dunkirk ends as German forces seize the city; Winston Churchill makes his famous speech 'we shall fight them on the beaches'.

**Wednesday 5:** Germany steps up the invasion of France, attacking across the Somme and Aisne rivers.

**Thursday 6:** The French army temporarily halts the German advance at Oisemont.

**Friday 7:** Singer Tom Jones is born in Treforest, Wales; singer Nancy Sinatra is born in Jersey City, New Jersey.

**Saturday 8:** The German 5th Panzer Division captures the French city of Rouen. All Allied troops are evacuated from Norway.

**Sunday 9:** The French government flees Paris and retreats to Tours in central France.

# June 1940

**Monday 10:** Benito Mussolini announces that Italy will join the war on the German side at midnight. Norway surrenders to Germany; King Haakon VII and his cabinet escape to London to form a government in exile.

**Tuesday 11:** Italian forces begin the Siege of Malta, bombing and cutting off supplies to the tiny British island in the Mediterranean.

**Wednesday 12:** 46,000 outflanked British and French troops surrender to the Germans at Saint-Valery-En-Caux.

**Thursday 13:** The Anglo-French Supreme War Council meets for the last time. Paris is declared an open city; Churchill urges the French to continue the fight from their north African colonies.

**Friday 14:** The Germans enter Paris unopposed.

**Saturday 15:** The French fortress of Verdun, which famously held out against the Germans in the First World War, capitulates.

**Sunday 16:** French Prime Minister Paul Reynaud resigns and is replaced by Phillipe Pétain, who begins surrender negotiations with Germany one hour after taking office.

A British tank in Malta with distinctive rock camouflage.

**Monday 17:** 4,000 allied servicemen die when the troopship RMS *Lancastria* is sunk off the French coast; it is the largest single loss of life on any British vessel in history.

**Tuesday 18:** France's General Charles de Gaulle makes his 'Appeal of 18 June' on the BBC, calling for the establishment of the French Resistance.

**Wednesday 19:** The British Jockey Club announces all horse racing will cease for the duration of the war.

**Thursday 20:** The Germans capture Lyons, France's second city.

Hitler visits Paris.

**Friday 21:** Surrender negotiations begin between France and Germany, personally attended by Adolf Hitler in the same railway carriage in the same railway sidings in which the Germans accepted the Armistice in 1918.

**Saturday 22:** The armistice between France and Germany is signed at 6.36pm; a German occupation zone is agreed for the north of the country with a 'free' south controlled by a French puppet government in Vichy.

**Sunday 23:** Adolf Hitler makes a victory tour of Paris. The BBC's programme *Music While You Work* is first broadcast.

# June 1940

**Monday 24:** The Franco-Italian armistice is signed, with a small zone of occupation granted to the Italians at Menton.

**Tuesday 25:** British commandos have a minor victory with Operation Collar near Calais, the first of several guerilla raids.

**Wednesday 26:** The Soviet Union abandons the use of its 'eternal calendar' of five day weeks with no weekends (introduced in 1929), returning to the standard seven day week.

**Thursday 27:** Britain announces a blockade of the European coastline from the south of France to the north of Norway.

**Friday 28:** 42 people are killed in German air raids on Britain's Channel Islands of Jersey and Guernsey.

**Saturday 29:** The Alien Registration Act (the Smith Act) is passed in the USA.

**Sunday 30:** German forces occupy the Channel Islands unopposed. It is the only part of the British Isles to come under German control during the war.

**Germans occupy the British Channel Islands.**

# July 1940

The Tacoma Narrows Bridge opens.

**Monday 1:** The Tacoma Narrows Bridge, the third longest suspension bridge in the world at this date, opens in Washington.

**Tuesday 2:** 865 people are killed when the British ship *Arandora Star*, carrying German and Italian internees from Britain to camps in Canada, is sunk by a German U-boat.

**Wednesday 3:** The RAF bombs the French fleet in Algeria to prevent its use by the Vichy government. The Cardiff Blitz begins as German planes bomb the Welsh capital.

**Thursday 4:** The film *All this, and Heaven Too* starring Bette Davis and Charles Boyer is released in the USA.

**Friday 5:** Vichy France severs diplomatic links with Britain following the attack on the French fleet.

**Saturday 6:** German bombers attack the city of Plymouth in south west England. The Story Bridge opens in Brisbane, Australia.

**Sunday 7:** Ringo Starr, drummer with The Beatles, is born in Liverpool, England.

# July 1940

**Monday 8:** Germany signs an agreement with neutral Sweden to allow war supplies to pass through the country.

**Tuesday 9:** The Duke of Windsor, (formerly King Edward VIII, who abdicated in 1936), is appointed Governor of the Bahamas.

**Wednesday 10:** The Battle of Britain begins. The Luftwaffe attacks British coastal defences in preparation for a seaborne invasion.

**Thursday 11:** The British government confirms that the Ethiopian government under Emperor Haile Selassi (in exile in British Mandatory Palestine) is an ally and that Ethiopia will be granted independence after the war.

**Friday 12:** US inventor Frederick McKinley Jones, co-founder of the Thermo King company, registers a patent for the first air-conditioned food transport truck.

**Saturday 13:** Actor Patrick Stewart (Captain Picard in *Star Trek*) is born in Mirfield, England.

**Sunday 14:** Bastille Day (the commemoration of the 1789 French Revolution) in Vichy France is observed solemnly, with flags at half mast.

**RAF pilots 'scramble' at Duxford during the Battle of Britain.**

# July 1940

**Monday 15:** The Brighton Blitz begins as German planes attack England's major south coast holiday resort. France's eastern regions of Alsace and Lorraine are annexed by Germany. Robert Wadlow, the world's tallest man, dies aged 22.

**Robert Wadlow, the world's tallest man (8ft 11 ins) dies aged 22.**

**Tuesday 16:** Adolf Hitler authorises the invasion of England, code-named Operation Sealion. Despite extensive preparations the plans are shelved in September after Germany's failure to destroy the Royal Air Force.

**Wednesday 17:** Comedian Tim Brooke-Taylor (*The Goodies, I'm Sorry I Haven't a Clue*) is born in Buxton, Derbyshire, England.

**Thursday 18:** Franklin D. Roosevelt is nominated to serve for an unprecedented third term as US President.

**Comedian Tim Brooke-Taylor.**

**Friday 19:** Following Britain's refusal to accept peace terms, Hitler announces he will have no option but to destroy the British Empire.

**Saturday 20:** The buying and selling of new cars is prohibited in the United Kingdom.

**Sunday 21:** Following rigged elections, the Soviet Socialist Republics of Estonia, Lithuania and Latvia are established.

# July 1940

**Monday 22:** Britain's Special Operations Executive (SOE) is formed to carry out espionage and sabotage in foreign occupied countries.

**Tuesday 23:** Britain's armed civilian militia, the Local Defence Volunteers, is renamed the Home Guard at the suggestion of Winston Churchill.

**A Home Guard sergeant cleans his Thompson gun at home with his wife in Dorking, Surrey.**

**Wednesday 24:** Members of the Californian religious cult 'I AM' are tried for fraud after claiming that Jesus Christ sat for a portrait by one of their members, artist Charles Sindelar.

**Thursday 25:** John Sigmund begins a record breaking swim of 292 miles down the Mississippi River, which takes 89 hours 46 minutes.

**Friday 26:** *Pride and Prejudice,* starring Greer Garson and Laurence Olivier, is released in the USA.

**Saturday 27:** *Billboard* magazine begins to list the top-selling records in the USA. The first 'number one' is *I'll Never Smile Again* by Tommy Dorsey and his Orchestra.

**Sunday 28:** Germany's top fighter pilot Werner Mölders is put out of the Battle of Britain after being badly wounded.

# July/August 1940

**Monday 29:** Germany postpones the planned invasion of Russia to 1941.

**Tuesday 30:** British inventor Sir Clive Sinclair, inventor of the first slimline calculator, the ZX81 home computer and the C5 electric tricycle, is born in Richmond, Surrey.

**Wednesday 31:** Britain begins Operation Hurry, the transfer of aircraft to the island of Malta. TV personality Roy Walker (*Catchphrase*) is born in Belfast, Northern Ireland.

**General de Gaulle.**

**Thursday 1:** Charles de Gaulle, head of the Free French government in exile, makes a radio appeal for help from French Canadians.

**Friday 2:** A military court in Vichy France tries Charles de Gaulle *in absentia* and sentences him to death.

**Saturday 3:** The Italian army invades British Somaliland. Actor Martin Sheen (*Apocalypse Now*, *The West Wing*) is born in Dayton, Ohio.

**Sunday 4:** America's General John Pershing makes a radio address urging aid to be sent to Britain. On the same day, pilot Charles Lindbergh makes an appeal for isolationism.

**Above left: Roy Walker. Above right: Martin Sheen.**

# August 1940

**Monday 5:** Italian forces capture the city of Zeila in British Somaliland.

**Tuesday 6:** The US ambassador to Belgium reports that food stocks in Belgium and France are desperately low with occupying German forces making no attempt to solve the problem.

**Wednesday 7:** The cathedral city of Exeter in south west England is bombed for the first time.

**Thursday 8:** Jazz clarinetist Johnny Dodds, best known for his recordings with Louis Armstrong, 'King' Oliver and Jelly Roll Morton, dies aged 48.

**Friday 9:** The Birmingham Blitz begins as the first air raid takes place on Britain's second largest city.

**Saturday 10:** The British armed merchant cruiser *Transylvania* is sunk by German submarine U-56 off the Scottish coast.

**Sunday 11:** 50 people are killed when a hurricane hits the coasts of Georgia and South Carolina.

**Bomb damage in Aston Newtown, Birmingham, including a bent but intact metal Anderson air raid shelter.**

# August 1940

**Monday 12:** The Battle of Britain intensifies as German planes bomb radar installations on England's south coast. Food wastage is made illegal in the UK.

**Tuesday 13:** Three members of the Australian cabinet are among the ten fatalities in the Canberra air disaster when a Lockheed Hudson aeroplane crash lands near the Australian capital.

**Wednesday 14:** The US government approves emergency plans for the defence of the western hemisphere, code-named Rainbow Number Four.

**Thursday 15:** The largest engagement so far in the Battle of Britain takes place; the Germans lose 76 aircraft to Britain's 34, leading the Germans to christen it Black Thursday.

RAF Supermarine Spitfires flying in formation during the Battle of Britain.

**Friday 16:** 48 volunteers make the first US army parachute jump in a training exercise.

**Saturday 17:** Adolf Hitler orders a total blockade of Great Britain.

**Sunday 18:** The largest aerial engagement in history takes place in the Battle of Britain. Known as 'the hardest day', both sides lose more aircraft on this than any other day.

# August 1940

**Monday 19:** Italian troops capture the city of Berbera in British Somaliland.

**Tuesday 20:** Winston Churchill makes his 'never was so much owed by so many to so few' speech about the Battle of Britain.

**Wednesday 21:** Soviet exile Leon Trotsky dies after being attacked with an icepick in Mexico City the previous day.

**Thursday 22:** The first bomb of the war falls on London, hitting the suburb of Harrow at 3.30 am.

**Friday 23:** King George VI commands that all Germans and Italians are to be stripped of British decorations. Benito Mussolini loses his Order of the Bath presented in 1923.

**Saturday 24:** German bombs fall on the City of London and the West End; Churchill orders a retaliatory attack on Berlin.

**Sunday 25:** The RAF carries out an air raid on Berlin, causing humiliation for Luftwaffe chief Hermann Göring, who boasted that the city would never be bombed.

**Above: poster for the Battle of Britain. Above right: Germany's air force chief Hermann Göring.**

# August/September 1940

**Monday 26:** Three people are killed when the Luftwaffe bombs a dairy in the village of Campile, County Wexford in neutral Eire. Rumours abound that the attack is a warning, as the dairy had been supplying food to Britain.

**Tuesday 27:** A bloodless coup in the French colony of Cameroon transfers the country from Vichy allegiance to control by the Free French.

**Wednesday 28:** The Liverpool Blitz begins.

**Thursday 29:** Germany formally apologises to Eire for the Wexford bombing.

**Friday 30:** Germany returns Northern Transylvania (assigned to Romania at the Treaty of Versailles in 1920) to Hungary.

**Saturday 31:** Film stars Laurence Olivier and Vivien Leigh are married at San Ysidro Ranch, California.

**Sunday 1:** The major RAF base at Biggin Hill aerodrome in Kent, southern England, is badly damaged in a German air raid.

**Left: three WRAF telephonists received the Military Medal for gallantry following the attack on Biggin Hill aerodrome, keeping vital telephone lines open despite heavy bombing.**

# September 1940

**Monday 2:** The US government agrees to trade old American destroyers for 99-year leases on British bases.

**Tuesday 3:** Adolf Hitler fixes the date of Operation Sealion, the invasion of England, for 21 September.

**Wednesday 4:** The America First Committee is established, with the aim of keeping the USA out of the war.

**Thursday 5:** Actress Raquel Welch (*One Million Years BC*) is born in Chicago, Illinois.

**Friday 6:** Following serious unrest in Romania due to the loss of territory to Hungary, the unpopular King Carol II abdicates in favour of his son, Michael.

**Saturday 7:** The London Blitz begins. Former French Prime Ministers Édouard Daladier and Paul Reynaud are arrested and interned without trial in Paris.

**Sunday 8:** Jayachamarajendra Wadiyar is crowned Maharaja of the Indian kingdom of Mysore.

A civilian volunteer watches for enemy aircraft over the City of London.

# September 1940

**Monday 9:** Italy invades Egypt; the Italian air force bombs Tel Aviv in British Mandatory Palestine, killing 137.

**Tuesday 10:** The Italian Air Force enters the Battle of Britain.

**Wednesday 11:** Winston Churchill warns on the radio that the invasion of England may be imminent, ordering that 'every man and woman will therefore prepare himself and herself to do his duty whatever it may be.'

**Thursday 12:** Some of the best examples of prehistoric cave paintings are discovered at Lascaux near Montignac, France.

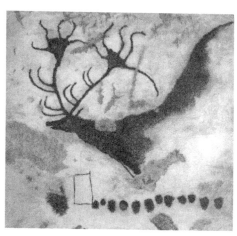

**Left: a prehistoric cave painting of a giant deer (*Megaloceros*), one of many discovered at Lascaux, France.**

**Friday 13:** Italian forces invade Libya. Buckingham Palace in London is bombed; the King and Queen, who have refused to leave the city, are unhurt.

**Saturday 14:** The RAF carries out a heavy bombing raid on the Belgian city of Antwerp.

**Sunday 15:** Battle of Britain Day: the Luftwaffe mounts an all-out offensive, sending 250 bombers to attack London. The RAF shoots down 61, inflicting a decisive defeat.

# September 1940

**Monday 16:** The Selective Training and Service Act 1940 is passed in the USA, introducing peacetime conscription for the first time.

**Tuesday 17:** Following the rout of the Luftwaffe on 15 September, Hitler postpones the invasion of England (Operation Sealion) indefinitely.

**Wednesday 18:** 77 evacuee children are killed when the British passenger ship SS *City of Benares* is torpedoed by a German U-boat. Following a public outcry, Winston Churchill orders the cancellation of the Canadian evacuation programme.

**Thursday 19:** The RAF bombs the German invasion barges on the French coast prepared for the invasion of England.

**Friday 20:** The Universal horror film *The Mummy's Hand* starring Peggy Moran is released in the USA.

**Saturday 21:** The British government officially approves the use of London Underground stations as air raid shelters.

**Sunday 22:** Japanese troops invade French Indochina.

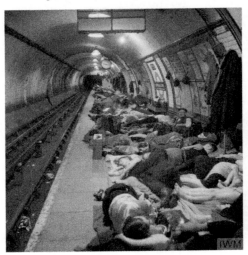

**The British government officially approves the use of London Underground stations as air raid shelters. Left: Londoners sleep at Elephant and Castle station on the Northern Line.**

# September 1940

**Monday 23:** King George VI announces the creation of two civilian medals, the George Cross and the George Medal.

**Tuesday 24:** Vichy French aeroplanes bomb the British colony of Gibraltar. Jimmie Foxx becomes only the second player in major league baseball history (after Babe Ruth) to score 500 home runs.

**Wednesday 25:** Germany bans all political parties in Norway apart from Vidkung Quisling's Nasjonal Samling party. 'Quisling' becomes a byword for 'collaborator' in Britain.

**Thursday 26:** Welsh Poet and travel writer William Henry Davies (*Autobiography of a Super Tramp*) dies aged 69.

**Friday 27:** Germany, Italy and Japan sign the Tripartite Pact for military co-operation.

The 'Battle' of Graveney Marsh takes place in Kent, England. A short skirmish between the London Irish Rifles and the crew of a downed German bomber, it is the first exchange of fire between British and foreign forces on British soil since 1797.

**Saturday 28:** The Belgian government in exile in London begins broadcasting Radio Belgique to German occupied Belgium.

**Sunday 29:** Two Avro Anson aircraft of the Royal Australian Air Force collide in mid air over New South Wales, Australia. Miraculously, nobody is hurt as the planes lock together and both are able to land safely.

**Above: the two RAAF Avro Ansons locked together.**

# September/October 1940

**Monday 30:** Unofficial evacuation of schoolchildren from Berlin begins.

*Wait for me, Daddy:* **Claude P. Dettloff's famous photograph of The British Columbia Regiment.**

**Tuesday 1:** The famous photograph of departing Canadian soldiers, *Wait for me Daddy*, is taken by photographer Claude P Dettloff in New Westminster, British Columbia.

**Wednesday 2:** The Pennsylvania Turnpike, the first high-speed toll controlled road in the USA, opens.

**Thursday 3:** Vichy France passes anti-semitic legislation, barring Jews from most occupations.

**Friday 4:** Fritzie Zivic defeats Henry Armstrong to win the world welterweight boxing title at Madison Square Garden, New York City.

**Saturday 5:** Ballington Booth, son of Salvation Army founder William Booth and founder of the charity Volunteers of America, dies aged 83.

**Sunday 6:** The North Atlantic Convoy vessel *Benlawers* is sunk with the loss of 24 crew.

# October 1940

**Monday 7:** The RAF conducts its heaviest air raid on Berlin to date.

**Tuesday 8:** German troops enter Romania.

**Wednesday 9:** Singer-songwriter John Lennon of the Beatles is born in Liverpool, England (died 1980).

**Thursday 10:** Germany begins building air raid shelters across the country; it is the largest public works programme in history.

**Friday 11:** The technicolor musical *Down Argentine Way* is released in the USA, introducing singer Carmen Miranda.

**Saturday 12:** Film star Tom Mix, the first screen cowboy, dies in a car accident aged 60.

**Sunday 13:** The 14 year old Princess Elizabeth, heir to the British throne, makes her first public speech in a radio address to the children of the British Empire.

**Top left: John Lennon. Above left: Tom Mix. Above right: Carmen Miranda.**

# October 1940

**Monday 14:** 66 people are killed when a bomb hits Balham underground station in south London. Singer Sir Cliff Richard is born in Lucknow, India.

**Tuesday 15:** Charlie Chaplin's satirical comedy film *The Great Dictator* premieres in New York City.

**Wednesday** 16: US officials raid the territory of the O'odham tribe in Arizona after members of the Indian tribe refuse to register for military service.

**Thursday 17:** American self-help writer and New Thought practitioner Florence Scovell Shinn (*The Game of Life and How to Play It*) dies aged 69.

**Friday 18:** 20 out of the 35 ships in North Atlantic Convoy SC7 are sunk by a U-boat wolfpack west of Ireland.

**Saturday 19:** *Only Forever* by Bing Crosby hits number one in the US charts. Actor Sir Michael Gambon (Dumbledore in the *Harry Potter* films) is born in Dublin, Eire.

**Sunday 20:** SS leader Heinrich Himmler visits Spanish dictator Francisco Franco for talks in Madrid.

**Chaplin stars in *The Great Dictator* as Adenoid Hynkel, the authoritarian leader of Tomainia.**

# October 1940

**Monday 21:** Ernest Hemingway's novel *For Whom the Bell Tolls* is published.

**Tuesday 22:** Hitler meets senior French Vichy politician Pierre Laval for talks in Montoire-sur-le-Loir.

**Wednesday 23:** Francisco Franco, dictator of Spain, meets Adolf Hitler for seven hours of discussion at Hendaye on the Franco-Spanish border, during which Hitler fails to convince Franco to bring neutral Spain into the war on the German side.

Footballer Pelé is born in Três Corações, Brazil.

**Thursday 24:** Hitler meets with Philippe Pétain, Prime Minister of Vichy France, who agrees to collaborate with, (but not formally join) the German side.

**Friday 25:** Benjamin O Davis Sr becomes the first black general in the US Army.

**Saturday 26:** The US P-51 Mustang fighter makes its first flight.

**Top: Hitler meets Franco.
Above: The P51 Mustang.**

**Sunday 27:** Italy's ambassador to Greece issues an ultimatum demanding that Italian troops be allowed to occupy the country.

# October/November 1940

**Monday 28:** Following Prime Minister Ioannis Metaxas' rejection of Italy's ultimatum, the Italian invasion of Greece begins. Hitler is reportedly furious, claiming Malta should have been invaded instead.

**Tuesday 29:** Britain occupies the Greek island of Crete.

**Wednesday 30:** Philippe Pétain, Prime Minister of Vichy France, announces on French radio that he has decided to collaborate with Germany 'to maintain French unity'.

**A Greek woman gives her son an icon before he departs for the front.**

**Thursday 31:** The Battle of Britain ends, with the Luftwaffe's total losses amounting to 2375 planes to Britain's 800.

**Friday 1:** Following the Italian invasion of Greece, Turkey declares neutrality.

**Saturday 2:** Greek air force pilot Marinos Mitralexis, after his plane runs out of fuel, rams an Italian air force bomber, causing the crew to bail out and the plane to crash land. Mitralexis lands his own plane and proceeds to capture the Italian crew single-handedly.

**Sunday 3:** After 57 consecutive nights of bombing, London enjoys a night without attack.

# November 1940

**Monday 4:** The Royal Navy begins Operation MB8 to protect Mediterranean convoys.

**Tuesday 5:** Franklin D Roosevelt wins an unprecedented third term in the USA's Presidential elections.

**Wednesday 6:** British, Sudanese and Indian troops engage the Italian army in the Sudan.

**Thursday 7:** The Tacoma Narrows Bridge in Washington (nicknamed 'galloping gertie' due to its alarming movements in high winds) collapses just four months after opening.

**Friday 8:** The Battle of Gabon, the war's only significant engagement in central Africa, begins as Free French and Vichy French forces clash in Libreville.

**Saturday 9:** Neville Chamberlain, former Prime Minister of the United Kingdom, dies aged 71.

**Sunday 10:** The Copacabana nightclub, immortalised in the song of the same name by Barry Manilow, opens in New York City.

Roosevelt on the campaign trail.

# November 1940

**Monday 11:** The Royal Navy attacks the Italian fleet at Taranto; it is the first battle in which an aircraft carrier uses its planes to attack ships.

**Tuesday 12:** Allied forces are victorious in Taranto, Gabon and the Straits of Otranto.

**Wednesday 13:** The Walt Disney Mickey Mouse feature film *Fantasia*, the first major film with stereo sound, premieres in the USA.

**Most of the historic city centre of Coventry is destroyed.**

**Thursday 14:** The most devastating attacks of the Coventry Blitz take place as 515 German bombers attack the English midlands city; at 8pm the city's medieval cathedral is hit by incendiary bombs and soon burnt to the ground.

**Friday 15:** Comedy duo Abbott and Costello make their screen debut in *One Night in the Tropics*.

**Saturday 16:** Nazi authorities seal the Warsaw Ghetto, forcing 380,000 Jews to stay inside.

**Sunday 17:** English sculptor and printmaker Eric Gill, designer of the Gill Sans typeface, dies aged 58.

# November 1940

**Monday 18:** The Germans expel 100,000 French citizens from the Lorraine region of France, now part of Germany.

**Tuesday 19:** Approximately 900 people are killed during a major bombing raid in the Birmingham Blitz.

**Wednesday 20:** Hungary joins the Axis forces.

**Thursday 21:** Greek forces push the Italian army back into Albania.

**Friday 22:** Animator Terry Gilliam of the Monty Python comedy team is born in Minneapolis, Minnesota.

**Saturday 23:** 77 people are killed in a bombing raid on the southern English port city of Southampton. Romania joins the Axis forces.

**Sunday 24:** The Bristol Blitz begins as the Luftwaffe attacks the largest city in the west of England. The Slovak Republic joins the Axis forces.

**Children being evacuated from Bristol.**

# November/December 1940

**Monday 25:** The Jewish paramilitary organisation Haganah bombs the ocean liner *Patria*, intending to wreck the engines to prevent it leaving Haifa with c.1800 Jewish refugees who have been refused entry to British Mandatory Palestine. The bombers miscalculate, however, and the ship sinks with the loss of 267 lives. British authorities allow the survivors to remain on humanitarian grounds.

Woody Woodpecker makes his first screen appearance in the cartoon *Knock Knock.*

**Tuesday 26:** In Nazi-Soviet negotations the USSR indicates it is willing to join the Axis side if certain territorial demands are met, including the annexation of Finland; Hitler refuses the demands.

**Wednesday 27:** Martial arts expert and actor Bruce Lee is born in San Francisco, California (died 1973).

**Thursday 28:** 166 people are killed when a German bomb hits an air raid shelter in Durning Road, Liverpool, north west England. Prime Minister Winston Churchill calls it 'the worst civilian incident of the war.'

**Bruce Lee.**

**Friday 29:** Following the breakdown of Nazi-Soviet talks, the German high command issues a plan for the invasion of the USSR.

**Saturday 30:** 137 people are killed in a six-hour bombing raid on Southampton, England.

**Sunday 1:** Comedian Richard Pryor is born Peoria, Illinois (died 2005).

**Richard Pryor.**

# December 1940

**Monday 2:** British armed merchant cruiser *Forfar* is sunk by German submarine U-99 west of Scotland.

**Tuesday 3:** Greek forces capture the Albanian port of Sarandë from the Italians.

**Wednesday 4:** 500 Italians are taken prisoner when the Greek army captures Përmet in southern Albania.

**Thursday 5:** The technicolor fantasy film *The Thief of Baghdad,* produced by Alexander Korda and directed by Michael Powell, is released in the USA.

**Friday 6:** Dino Alfieri, Italian ambassador to Berlin, is given a stern warning by German foreign minister Joachim von Ribentropp about Italy's mishandling of the invasion of Greece; Field Marshal Pietro Badoglio, head of the Italian army, is forced to resign.

**Saturday 7:** The British Fairey Barracuda dive bomber, the replacement for the obsolete Fairey Swordfish biplane, makes its first flight.

**A Fairey Barracuda armed with a torpedo.**

**Sunday 8:** The Chicago Bears beat the Washington Redskins 73-0 in the National Football League (NFL) championship game in Washington, DC. It remains the worst defeat in NFL history.

# December 1940

**Monday 9:** The Allies begin Operation Compass, the first major engagement of the war in the north African desert.

**Tuesday 10:** The Battle of Sidi Barrani begins as British forces attempt to retake the Egyptian port of Sidi Barrani.

**Wednesday 11:** The Battle of Sidi Barrani ends in British victory and the capture of large numbers of Italian prisoners.

**Thursday 12:** The Sheffield Blitz begins, as German bombers attack the industrial city of Sheffield in Yorkshire, northern England.

**Friday 13:** French minister of state Pierre Laval is dismissed by the Prime Minister Philippe Pétain for collaborating too closely with the Germans. Laval's defence is that the Vichy government is powerless to stop the Germans doing anything they please.

**Saturday 14:** The element Plutonium is isolated and produced for the first time, at the University of California, Berkeley.

**Sunday 15:** The ashes of France's Emperor Napoleon II, who died in Austria in 1832, are ceremonially brought to to Paris for burial, in a gesture intended by Hitler to assuage the French.

Italian prisoners are marched from Sidi Barrani.

# December 1940

**Monday 16:** The first area bombardment (bombing of a general area rather than a specific target) of a German city takes place, as the RAF attacks the city of Mannheim in southwestern Germany.

**Tuesday 17:** Dorothy O'Grady becomes the first Briton to be convicted of treason in the war, after being caught making drawings of coastal defences. She is sentenced to death (later commuted to 14 years imprisonment).

**Wednesday 18:** Adolf Hitler issues his secret personal plans for the invasion of the USSR, codenamed Operation Barbarossa.

**Thursday 19:** The German submarine *U-37* accidentally sinks the Vichy French submarine *Sfax* off the coast of Morocco.

**Friday 20:** Issue number one of *Captain America* comics is published in the USA, marking the first appearance of Captain America.

**Saturday 21:** Author F Scott Fitzgerald (*The Great Gatsby*) dies aged 44.

**Sunday 22:** German bombers attack England's northwestern industrial city of Manchester. 363 people are killed and Manchester Cathedral is badly damaged.

**Devastation in Manchester.**

# December 1940

**Monday 23:** Winston Churchill broadcasts an appeal to the people of Italy, calling for them to overthrow Mussolini for bringing them into a war against their wishes.

**Tuesday 24:** Mahatma Gandhi writes to Adolf Hitler, addressing him as 'dear friend' and appealing to him to end the war.

**Wednesday 25:** The Rodgers and Hart stage musical *Pal Joey* starring Gene Kelly premieres on Broadway.

**Thursday 26:** The romantic comedy film *The Philadelphia Story* starring Cary Grant, Katharine Hepburn and James Stewart is released in the USA.

**Friday 27:** Grand Admiral Erich Raeder, chief of the German fleet, meets with Adolf Hitler in Berlin to express 'grave doubts' about starting a war with the USSR.

**Saturday 28:** This is the only day of the entire month that no allied shipping is lost due to enemy action.

Poster for *The Philadelphia Story*.

**Sunday 29:** Heavy incendiary bombing causes major fires to break out all over the City of London, causing an American journalist to describe it as the 'Second Great Fire of London'.

# December 1940

**Monday 30:** In the early hours of the morning, photographer Herbert Mason takes his iconic photograph *St Paul's Survives,* of London's St Paul's Cathedral undamaged but surrounded by fire and smoke.

Rumours abound of divine intervention or that Hitler ordered the cathedral to be spared; it is more likely that the building was saved by its dedicated team of volunteer firemen who at great risk to their own safety protected it from 29 incendiary bombs.

**Tuesday 31:** Adolf Hitler announces to Germany's armed forces that 1941 'will bring us, on the Western Front, the completion of the greatest victory of our history'.

*St Paul's Survives* by Herbert Mason. Mason took the photograph from the roof of the *Daily Mail*'s offices on Fleet Street while on duty as a volunteer fire warden.

# Birthday Notebooks
## ...a great alternative to a card.

Handy 60 page ruled notebooks with a significant event from the year heading each page.

**Available from Montpelier Publishing at Amazon.**

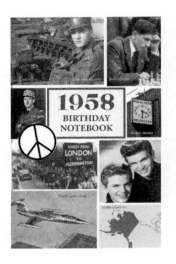

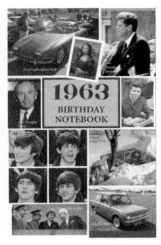

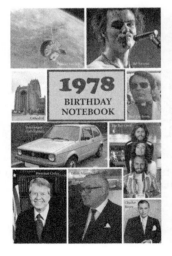

Printed in Great Britain
by Amazon